Air Fryer Cookbook With Colorful Pictures 2023 UK

1200 Days of Low-Calorie, Affordable & Healthy Recipes for Beginners, Perfect for Frying with Less Oil

Elise Fowler

CONTENTS

Introduction 4

Chapter 1 Introducing the Air Fryer 4

Getting Acquainted with Air Frying 4
How air frying works 5
Different models on the market 5
Seeing the benefits of air frying 6

Measurement Conversions 8

Chapter 2 Breakfast & Snacks And Fries Recipes 10

Raspberry Breakfast Pockets 11
Wholegrain Pitta Chips 11
Easy Cheese & Bacon Toasties 12
Potato Fries 12
Breakfast Doughnuts 13
Healthy Stuffed Peppers 13
Courgette Fries 14
Healthy Breakfast Bagels 14
Oozing Baked Eggs 15
French Toast Slices 15
Mexican Breakfast Burritos 16
Egg & Bacon Breakfast Cups 16
Breakfast Sausage Burgers 17
Delicious Breakfast Casserole 17
Easy Air Fryer Sausage 18
Potato & Chorizo Frittata 18
Muhammara 19

Chapter 3 Beef & Lamb And Pork Recipes 20

Breaded Bone-in Pork Chops 21
Meatballs In Tomato Sauce 21
Pork Chops With Sprouts 22
Roast Beef 22
Meatloaf 23
Copycat Burger 23

Mustard Glazed Pork 24
Traditional Pork Chops 24
Pork Schnitzel....25
Beef Wellington 25
Homemade Crispy Pepperoni Pizza....26
Asparagus & Steak Parcels....27
Steak Popcorn Bites 28
Hamburgers With Feta 28
Beef Stuffed Peppers 29
Pork Belly With Crackling 30

Chapter 4 Poultry Recipes....31

Bacon Wrapped Chicken Thighs 32
Smoky Chicken Breast 33
Charred Chicken Breasts 33
Pizza Chicken Nuggets 34
Turkey Cutlets In Mushroom Sauce 35
Whole Chicken 35
Chicken Kiev....36
Crunchy Chicken Tenders 37
Chicken Balls, Greek-style 37
Air Fried Maple Chicken Thighs 38
Chicken Tikka 38
Chicken And Cheese Chimichangas 39
Chicken Tikka Masala....39
Grain-free Chicken Katsu 40
Sticky Chicken Tikka Drumsticks....41
Hawaiian Chicken....41
Nashville Chicken....42

Chapter 5 Fish & Seafood Recipes....43

Chilli Lime Tilapia....44
Garlic-parsley Prawns 44
Crunchy Fish 45
Air Fryer Tuna....45
Mahi Fish Tacos....46
Honey Sriracha Salmon....47
Salt & Pepper Calamari....47
Ranch Style Fish Fillets....48
Copycat Fish Fingers....48
Baked Panko Cod....49
Cajun Prawn Skewers 49
Mushrooms Stuffed With Crab 50
Garlic Tilapia....50
Garlic Butter Salmon 51
Crispy Nacho Prawns....51

Tandoori Salmon....52
Zesty Fish Fillets....52

Chapter 6 Vegetarian & Vegan Recipes 53

Macaroni & Cheese Quiche....54
Roasted Cauliflower 54
Spinach And Egg Air Fryer Breakfast Muffins....55
Courgette Burgers 56
Ravioli Air Fryer Style 56
Chickpea And Sweetcorn Falafel....57
Camembert & Soldiers 58
Onion Dumplings....58
Flat Mushroom Pizzas....59
Air Fryer Cheese Sandwich....59
Pakoras 60
Roast Cauliflower & Broccoli 60
Lentil Burgers 61
Broccoli Cheese 61
Ratatouille....62
Roast Vegetables 62

Chapter 7 Desserts Recipes....63

Brazilian Pineapple....64
Key Lime Cupcakes....64
Chocolate Shortbread Balls....65
Thai Fried Bananas 65
Brownies....66
Chocolate Cake....66
Chocolate Dipped Biscuits....67
Zebra Cake....67
Apple Pie 68
Melting Moments 69
Christmas Biscuits....69
Apple And Cinnamon Puff Pastry Pies 70
Banana And Nutella Sandwich 71
Lava Cakes....71
Banana Maple Flapjack....72

Appendix : Recipes Index....73

INTRODUCTION

Whether you're an air fryer beginner or a veteran, you likely know that this small but mighty appliance has been revolutionizing kitchens everywhere for the past few years with no signs of slowing down. Air fryers continue to rise in popularity not only because they offer reduced cooking times and crispy food without all the oil and fat, but also because they can replace your oven, microwave, deep fryer, and dehydrator. All this saves you time, money, and precious counter space!

Using an air fryer saves time in its own right, and reducing the number of ingredients saves you even more. You don't need a pantry full of hard to find—or hard to pronounce—expensive ingredients in order to make quality meals. The same delicious flavors you love can be achieved with just five main ingredients (or less) and a handful of pantry staples. Developed for busy home cooks of all ages and skills, these recipes use simple preparations, wholesome and delicious ingredients, and best of all, lightning-fast cooking in your amazing air fryer.

Along with delicious recipes and mouthwatering photos, you'll find loads of kitchen hacks and flavoring suggestions to make cooking even more convenient and fitted to your preferences—there are so many ways to cut corners in the kitchen without cutting down on flavor!

Throughout this book you'll learn everything you need to know about using an air fryer, as well as helpful ways to elevate your meals—with only five ingredients—even if you're completely new to cooking. So let's get air frying!

Chapter 1 Introducing the Air Fryer

Getting Acquainted with Air Frying

When was the last time you enjoyed a decadent meal at a fair? You know the kind of food we're talking about: those greasy, fun foods you only get once every few years, the ones that bring you back to your childhood memories of late summer nights spent underneath the starlit sky with your best friends.

More often than not, the cooking method used to make those foods was deep frying. Although deep frying has its purposes (it's an efficient way to cook a large volume of food quickly), it isn't the best when it comes to health.

For years, engineers spent countless hours trying to come up with a user-friendly machine that would satisfy consumer desire for those rich and crispy fried foods, but they had a tough time replicating an appliance that could check all the boxes.

Everything changed in 2010 when a man with a vision, Fred van der Weij from Philips, finally saw it come to life, and the air fryer, as we've come to know it today, was born! Since then, many companies have brought similar air fryer models to market, designed to cook foods in a similar way.

In this section, we take a closer look into what air frying actually entails.

How air frying works

Have you ever seen one of those money machines, where someone steps inside a cylinder, closes the door, and air starts flowing up from the bottom with money flying through the air?

An air fryer is kind of like one of those money machines. When you put your food into the air fryer and close it, hot air circulates around the food and begins to cook it. The temperature of the air fryer and the type of food you're cooking will help determine the amount of time you need to cook your recipe.

The big difference between air frying and traditional deep frying is that air fryers require minimal to no oil to cook the food. The hot air circulating around the food helps to impart that crisp texture instead of the oil involved in deep frying.

A few other technologically advanced mechanisms are involved, but this is the gist of how air frying works.

If you're familiar with convection ovens, where hot air is circulated (as opposed to conventional ovens, where the heating element is on the bottom), you'll feel right at home with air frying. An air fryer is essentially a compact convection oven.

If you want to get a bit more science based, what's actually happening from a chemical perspective when food is cooked in an air fryer is something called the Maillard reaction. The Maillard reaction is often referred to as "non-enzymatic browning," or basically a reaction that happens between sugars and amino acids in a recipe that result in the end product taking on a new flavor, texture, and color.

Different models on the market

Just like most big kitchen appliances on the market today, the air fryer has lots of options. There is a make and model out there that will suit your needs and preferences. Here are the big factors that separate them:

Price: Air fryers can range anywhere from $50 to over $300, depending on what you're looking for. Air fryers at the higher end of the price range usually have more bells and whistles, as well as a higher wattage.

We've tested out $60 models and $200 models and can honestly say we've had similar experiences with both. Bottom line: You can produce a quality, air-fried food with any air fryer.

Size: Are you cooking for yourself? Two? Four? More? The more mouths you have to feed, the bigger the air fryer you'll want to look for.

Most models have about a 3- to 6-quart fill capacity, but some of the larger models on the market can hold up to 16 quarts. When you decide on how much counterspace you have and how many you'll typically be cooking for, you'll know the right model to choose.

Each of us has three mouths to feed in our homes and the 3-quart models work well for us. Plus, we've used 3-quart models before for entertaining family and friends and even with doubling the recipe, it still was efficient and quick to use.

Style of cooking: Say what? Yes, the type of cooking style will really be a huge deciding factor in choosing which model to buy. There are three main styles of air fryers you'll find on the market:

Paddle type: Typically, a self-turning fryer in which you add the cooking oil to the pan alongside the food.

Basket type: A drop-in basket that traditionally calls for multiple shakes within the cooking cycle. This type of air fryer requires a little more attention during the cooking process, but it's also a lot less expensive than the other varieties.

Countertop oven: This model resembles a toaster oven and has multiple uses. Depending on the make and model, they're fairly inexpensive and they usually allow for a greater volume of food to be cooked at one time than the basket types do.

We've tried the basket and countertop oven styles and found both fairly comparable. The only word of caution we have for the countertop oven models is this: Sometimes the heat doesn't disperse as evenly, requiring the items in the back of the air fryer to be rotated more frequently to avoid overcooking.

Seeing the benefits of air frying

Air frying is not only a healthier way to cook some more decadent recipes, but it's also efficient. Many popular models of air fryers claim that using an air fryer instead of a deep fryer can lower the fat of the dish by over 75 percent.

This actually makes sense when you think about. Let's say you're going to make homemade fried chicken. If you were to use the deep-frying method of cooking, you'd traditionally need more than 3 cups of oil to cover the chicken to allow the cooking to ensue. On the other hand, if you were to use the air frying method, you'd need less than a tablespoon of oil.

Not convinced yet? No problem! Here are a few other benefits of air frying:

Air fryers can promote weight loss (for certain individuals). For individuals who currently have a highly processed diet filled with deep-fried foods, switching to air frying will certainly help with reducing caloric intake. A reduction in caloric intake will inevitably result in weight loss.

Air fryers can increase consumption of healthy foods, like fish, shrimp, and produce. Eating seafood at least twice a week, as well as increasing your consumption of fruits and vegetables, is highly recommended. If you struggle with getting your family to eat more of these foods on a regular basis, then air frying may be the best way to change their appetites (and minds!).

Not only can you put a light crunchy coating of heart-healthy nuts on some of your fried seafood favorites and cook them in the air fryer, but you can do the same with new herbs, spices, and vegetables! This is a great way to explore new vegetables and flavors in your kitchen, too.

Air fryers are safer (for the most part) than deep fryers. Deep frying can cause splatters of exceptionally hot oil all over your kitchen. Air fryers get super-hot as well, but they don't splatter in the same way a deep fryer does.

Measurement Conversions

BASIC KITCHEN CONVERSIONS & EQUIVALENTS

DRY MEASUREMENTS CONVERSION CHART

3 TEASPOONS = 1 TABLESPOON = 1/16 CUP

6 TEASPOONS = 2 TABLESPOONS = 1/8 CUP

12 TEASPOONS = 4 TABLESPOONS = 1/4 CUP

24 TEASPOONS = 8 TABLESPOONS = 1/2 CUP

36 TEASPOONS = 12 TABLESPOONS = 3/4 CUP

48 TEASPOONS = 16 TABLESPOONS = 1 CUP

METRIC TO US COOKING CONVERSIONS

OVEN TEMPERATURES

120 °C = 250 °F

160 °C = 320 °F

180° C = 350 °F

205 °C = 400 °F

220 °C = 425 °F

LIQUID MEASUREMENTS CONVERSION CHART

8 FLUID OUNCES = 1 CUP = 1/2 PINT = 1/4 QUART

16 FLUID OUNCES = 2 CUPS = 1 PINT = 1/2 QUART

32 FLUID OUNCES = 4 CUPS = 2 PINTS = 1 QUART = 1/4 GALLON

128 FLUID OUNCES = 16 CUPS = 8 PINTS = 4 QUARTS = 1 GALLON

BAKING IN GRAMS

1 CUP FLOUR = 140 GRAMS

1 CUP SUGAR = 150 GRAMS

1 CUP POWDERED SUGAR = 160 GRAMS

1 CUP HEAVY CREAM = 235 GRAMS

VOLUME

1 MILLILITER = 1/5 TEASPOON

5 ML = 1 TEASPOON

15 ML = 1 TABLESPOON

240 ML = 1 CUP OR 8 FLUID OUNCES

1 LITER = 34 FL. OUNCES

WEIGHT

1 GRAM = .035 OUNCES

100 GRAMS = 3.5 OUNCES

500 GRAMS = 1.1 POUNDS

1 KILOGRAM = 35 OUNCES

US TO METRIC COOKING CONVERSIONS

1/5 TSP = 1 ML

1 TSP = 5 ML

1 TBSP = 15 ML

1 FL OUNCE = 30 ML

1 CUP = 237 ML

1 PINT (2 CUPS) = 473 ML

1 QUART (4 CUPS) = .95 LITER

1 GALLON (16 CUPS) = 3.8 LITERS

1 OZ = 28 GRAMS

1 POUND = 454 GRAMS

BUTTER

1 CUP BUTTER = 2 STICKS = 8 OUNCES = 230 GRAMS = 8 TABLESPOONS

WHAT DOES 1 CUP EQUAL

1 CUP = 8 FLUID OUNCES

1 CUP = 16 TABLESPOONS

1 CUP = 48 TEASPOONS

1 CUP = 1/2 PINT

1 CUP = 1/4 QUART

1 CUP = 1/16 GALLON

1 CUP = 240 ML

BAKING PAN CONVERSIONS

1 CUP ALL-PURPOSE FLOUR = 4.5 OZ

1 CUP ROLLED OATS = 3 OZ 1 LARGE EGG = 1.7 OZ

1 CUP BUTTER = 8 OZ 1 CUP MILK = 8 OZ

1 CUP HEAVY CREAM = 8.4 OZ

1 CUP GRANULATED SUGAR = 7.1 OZ

1 CUP PACKED BROWN SUGAR = 7.75 OZ

1 CUP VEGETABLE OIL = 7.7 OZ

1 CUP UNSIFTED POWDERED SUGAR = 4.4 OZ

BAKING PAN CONVERSIONS

9-INCH ROUND CAKE PAN = 12 CUPS

10-INCH TUBE PAN =16 CUPS

11-INCH BUNDT PAN = 12 CUPS

9-INCH SPRINGFORM PAN = 10 CUPS

9 X 5 INCH LOAF PAN = 8 CUPS

9-INCH SQUARE PAN = 8 CUPS

Chapter 2 Breakfast & Snacks And Fries Recipes

Raspberry Breakfast Pockets

Servings: 1

Ingredients:

- 2 slices of sandwich bread
- 1 tbsp soft cream cheese
- 1 tbsp raspberry jam
- 1 tbsp milk
- 1 egg

Directions:

1. Take one slice of the bread and add one tablespoon of jam into the middle
2. Take the second slice and add the cream cheese into the middle
3. Using a blunt knife, spread the jam and the cheese across the bread, but don't go to the outer edges
4. Take a small bowl and whisk the eggs and the milk together
5. Set your fryer to 190ºC and spray with a little oil
6. Dip your sandwich into the egg and arrange inside your fryer
7. Cook for 5 minutes on the first side, turn and cook for another 2 minutes

Wholegrain Pitta Chips

Servings: 2

Ingredients:

- 2 round wholegrain pittas, chopped into quarters
- 1 teaspoon olive oil
- ½ teaspoon garlic salt

Directions:

1. Preheat the air-fryer to 180ºC/350ºF.
2. Spray or brush each pitta quarter with olive oil and sprinkle with garlic salt. Place in the preheated air-fryer and air-fry for 4 minutes, turning halfway through cooking. Serve immediately.

Easy Cheese & Bacon Toasties

Servings: 2

Ingredients:

- 4 slices of sandwich bread
- 2 slices of cheddar cheese
- 5 slices of pre-cooked bacon
- 1 tbsp melted butter
- 2 slices of mozzarella cheese

Directions:

1. Take the bread and spread the butter onto one side of each slice
2. Place one slice of bread into the fryer basket, buttered side facing downwards
3. Place the cheddar on top, followed by the bacon, mozzarella and the other slice of bread on top, buttered side upwards
4. Set your fryer to 170ºC
5. Cook for 4 minutes and then turn over and cook for another 3 minutes
6. Serve whilst still hot

Potato Fries

Servings: 2

Ingredients:

- 2 large potatoes (baking potato size)
- 1 teaspoon olive oil
- salt

Directions:

1. Peel the potatoes and slice into fries about 5 x 1.5cm/¾ x ¾ in. by the length of the potato. Submerge the fries in a bowl of cold water and place in the fridge for about 10 minutes.
2. Meanwhile, preheat the air-fryer to 160ºC/325ºF.
3. Drain the fries thoroughly, then toss in the oil and season. Tip into the preheated air-fryer in a single layer (you may need to cook them in two batches, depending on the size of your air-fryer). Air-fry for 15 minutes, tossing once during cooking by shaking the air-fryer drawer, then increase the temperature of the air-fryer to 200ºC/400ºF and cook for a further 3 minutes. c.Serve immediately.

Breakfast Doughnuts

Servings:4

Ingredients:

- 1 packet of Pillsbury Grands
- 5 tbsp raspberry jam
- 1 tbsp melted butter
- 5 tbsp sugar

Directions:

1. Preheat your air fryer to 250ºC
2. Place the Pillsbury Grands into the air fryer and cook for around 5m minutes
3. Remove and place to one side
4. Take a large bowl and add the sugar
5. Coat the doughnuts in the melted butter, coating evenly
6. Dip into the sugar and coat evenly once more
7. Using an icing bag, add the jam into the bag and pipe an even amount into each doughnut
8. Eat warm or cold

Healthy Stuffed Peppers

Servings: 2

Ingredients:

- 1 large bell pepper, deseeded and cut into halves
- 1 tsp olive oil
- 4 large eggs
- Salt and pepper to taste

Directions:

1. Take your peppers and rub a little olive oil on the edges
2. Into each pepper, crack one egg and season with salt and pepper
3. You will need to insert a trivet into your air fryer to hold the peppers, and then arrange the peppers evenly
4. Set your fryer to 200ºC and cook for 13 minutes
5. Once cooked, remove and serve with a little more seasoning, if required

Courgette Fries

Servings: 2

Ingredients:

- 1 courgette/zucchini
- 3 tablespoons plain/all-purpose flour (gluten-free if you wish)
- ¼ teaspoon salt
- ¼ teaspoon freshly ground black pepper
- 60 g/¾ cup dried breadcrumbs (gluten-free if you wish; see page 9)
- 1 teaspoon dried oregano
- 20 g/¼ cup finely grated Parmesan

1 egg, beaten

Directions:

1. Preheat the air-fryer to 180ºC/350ºF.
2. Slice the courgette/zucchini into fries about 1.5 x 1.5 x 5 cm/⅝ x ⅝ x 2 in.
3. Season the flour with salt and pepper. Combine the breadcrumbs with the oregano and Parmesan.
4. Dip the courgettes/zucchini in the flour (shaking off any excess flour), then the egg, then the seasoned breadcrumbs.
5. Add the fries to the preheated air-fryer and air-fry for 15 minutes. They should be crispy on the outside but soft on the inside. Serve immediately.

Healthy Breakfast Bagels

Servings: 2

Ingredients:

- 170g self raising flour
- 120ml plain yogurt
- 1 egg

Directions:

1. Take a large mixing bowl, combine the flour and the yogurt to create a dough
2. Cover a flat surface with a little extra flour and set the dough down
3. Create four separate and even balls

d.Roll each ball out into a rope shape and form a bagel with each

4. Take a small mixing bowl and whisk the egg
5. Brush the egg over the top of the bagel
6. Arrange the bagels inside your fryer evenly
7. Cook at 170ºC for 10 minutes
8. Allow to cool before serving

Oozing Baked Eggs

Servings: 2

Ingredients:

- 4 eggs
- 140g smoked gouda cheese, cut into small pieces
- Salt and pepper to taste

Directions:

1 .You will need two ramekin dishes and spray each one before using
2 .Crack two eggs into each ramekin dish
3 .Add half of the Gouda cheese to each dish
4 .Season and place into the air fryer
5 .Cook at 350ºC for 15 minutes, until the eggs are cooked as you like them

French Toast Slices

Servings: 1

Ingredients:

- 2 eggs
- 5 slices sandwich bread
- 100ml milk
- 2 tbsp flour
- 3 tbsp sugar
- 1 tsp ground cinnamon
- 1/2 tsp vanilla extract
- Pinch of salt

Directions:

1 .Preheat your air fryer to 220ºC
2 .Take your bread and cut it into three pieces of the same size
3 .Take a mixing bowl and combine the other ingredients until smooth
4 .Dip the bread into the mixture, coating evenly
5 .Take a piece of parchment paper and lay it inside the air fryer
6 .Arrange the bread on the parchment paper in one layer
7 .Cook for 5 minutes
8 .Turn and cook for another 5 minutes

Mexican Breakfast Burritos

Servings: 6

Ingredients:

- 6 scrambled eggs
- 6 medium tortillas
- Half a minced red pepper
- 8 sausages, cut into cubes and browned
- 4 pieces of bacon, pre-cooked and cut into pieces
- 65g grated cheese of your choice
- A small amount of olive oil for cooking

Directions:

1 .Into a regular mixing bowl, combine the eggs, bell pepper, bacon pieces, the cheese, and the browned sausage, giving everything a good stir
2 .Take your first tortilla and place half a cup of the mixture into the middle, folding up the top and bottom and rolling closed
3 .Repeat until all your tortillas have been used
4 .Arrange the burritos into the bottom of your fryer and spray with a little oil
5 .Cook the burritos at 170ºC for 5 minutes

Egg & Bacon Breakfast Cups

Servings: 8

Ingredients:

- 6 eggs
- 1 chopped red pepper
- 1 chopped green pepper
- 1 chopped yellow pepper
- 2 tbsp double cream
- 50g chopped spinach
- 50g grated cheddar cheese
- 50g grated mozzarella cheese
- 3 slices of cooked bacon, crumbled into pieces

Directions:

1 .Take a large mixing bowl and crack the eggs
2 .Add the cream and season with a little salt and pepper, combining everything well
3 .Add the peppers, spinach, onions, both cheeses, and the crumbled bacon, combining everything once more
4 .You will need silicone moulds or cups for this part, and you should pour equal amounts of the mixture into 8 cups
5 .Cook at 150ºC for around 12 or 15 minutes, until the eggs are cooked properly

Breakfast Sausage Burgers

Servings: 2

Ingredients:

- 8 links of your favourite sausage
- Salt and pepper to taste

Directions:

1 .Remove the sausage from the skins and use a fork to create a smooth mixture
2 .Season to your liking
3 .Shape the sausage mixture into burgers or patties
4 .Preheat your air fryer to 260ºC
5 .Arrange the burgers in the fryer, so they are not touching each other
6 .Cook for 8 minutes
7 .Serve still warm

Delicious Breakfast Casserole

Servings: 4

Ingredients:

- 4 frozen hash browns
- 8 sausages, cut into pieces
- 4 eggs
- 1 diced yellow pepper
- 1 diced green pepper
- 1 diced red pepper
- Half a diced onion

Directions:

1 .Line the bottom of your fryer with aluminium foil and arrange the hash browns inside
2 .Add the sausage on top (uncooked)
3 .Now add the onions and the peppers, sprinkling evenly
4 .Cook the casserole on 170ºC for around 10 minutes
5 .Open your fryer and give the mixture a good stir
6 .Combine the eggs in a small bowl and pour over the casserole, closing the lid
7 .Cook for another 10 minutes on the same temperature
8 .Serve with a little seasoning to taste

Easy Air Fryer Sausage

Servings: 5

Ingredients:

- 5 uncooked sausages
- 1 tbsp mustard
- Salt and pepper for seasoning

Directions:

1 .Line the basket of your fryer with parchment paper
2 .Arrange the sausages inside the basket
3 .Set to 180ºC and cook for 15 minutes
4 .Turn the sausages over and cook for another 5 minutes
5 .Remove and cool
6 .Drizzle the mustard over the top and season to your liking

Potato & Chorizo Frittata

Servings: 2

Ingredients:

- 3 eggs
- 1 sliced chorizo sausage
- 1 potato, boiled and cubed
- 50g feta cheese
- 50g frozen sweetcorn
- A pinch of salt
- 1 tbsp olive oil

Directions:

1 .Add a little olive oil to the frying basket
2 .Add the corn, potato, and sliced chorizo to the basket
3 .Cook at 180ºC until the sausage is a little brown
4 .In a small bowl, beat together the eggs with a little seasoning
5 .Pour the eggs into the pan
6 .Crumble the feta on top
7 .Cook for 5 minutes
8 .Remove and serve in slices

Muhammara

Servings: 4

Ingredients:

- 4 romano peppers
- 4 tablespoons olive oil
- 100 g/1 cup walnuts
- 90 g/1 heaped cup dried breadcrumbs (see page 9)
- 1 teaspoon cumin
- 2 tablespoons pomegranate molasses
- freshly squeezed juice of ½ a lemon
- ½ teaspoon chilli/chili salt (or salt and some chilli/hot red pepper flakes combined)
- fresh pomegranate seeds, to serve

Directions:

1 .Preheat the air-fryer to 180ºC/350ºF.
2 .Rub the peppers with ½ teaspoon of the olive oil. Add the peppers to the preheated air-fryer and air-fry for 8 minutes.
3 .Meanwhile, lightly toast the walnuts by tossing them in a shallow pan over a medium heat for 3–5 minutes. Allow to cool, then grind the walnuts in a food processor. Once the peppers are cooked, chop off the tops and discard most of the seeds. Add to the food processor with all other ingredients. Process until smooth. Allow to cool in the fridge, then serve the dip with pomegranate seeds on top.

Chapter 3 Beef & Lamb And Pork Recipes

Meatballs In Tomato Sauce

Servings: 4

Ingredients:

- 1 small onion
- 300g minced pork
- 1 tbsp chopped parsley
- 1 tbsp thyme
- 1 egg
- 3 tbsp bread crumbs
- Salt and pepper to taste

Directions:

1 .Place all ingredients into a bowl and mix well
2 .Shape mixture into 12 meatballs
3 .Heat the air fryer to 200ºC
4 .Place the meatballs into the air fryer and cook for about 7 minutes
5 .Tip the meatballs into an oven dish add the tomato sauce and cook for about 5 minutes in the air fryer until warmed through

Breaded Bone-in Pork Chops

Servings: 2

Ingredients:

- 2 pork chops with the bone in
- 250g Italian breadcrumbs
- 2 tbsp mayonnaise
- 1/2 tsp garlic powder
- 1/2 tsp onion powder
- 1/2 tsp thyme
- 1/2 tsp paprika

Salt and pepper to taste

Directions:

1 .Preheat the air fryer to 260ºC
2 .Take a large bowl and add the breadcrumbs, garlic powder, paprika, salt and pepper, and thyme, and onion powder, combining well
3 .Cover the pork chops with the mayonnaise making sure to cover both sides
4 .Coat the meat with the seasoning mixture, making sure it is fully covered
5 .Cook the pork chops in the fryer for 10 minutes, turning over halfway

Pork Chops With Sprouts

Servings: 2

Ingredients:

• 300g pork chops
• ⅛ tsp salt
• ½ tsp pepper
• 250g Brussels sprouts quartered
• 1 tsp olive oil
• 1 tsp maple syrup
• 1 tsp dijon mustard

Directions:

1 .Season the pork chops with salt and pepper
2 .Mix together oil, maple syrup and mustard. Add Brussels sprouts
3 .Add pork chops and Brussels sprouts to the air fryer and cook at 200ºC for about 10 minutes

Roast Beef

Servings: 2

Ingredients:

• 400g beef fillet
• 1 tbsp olive oil
• 1 tsp salt
1 tsp rosemary

Directions:

1 .Preheat the air fryer to 180ºC
2 .Mix salt, rosemary and oil on a plate
3 .Coat the beef with the mix
4 .Place the beef in the air fryer and cook for 45 minutes turning halfway

Meatloaf

Servings: 2

Ingredients:

- 500g minced pork
- 1 egg
- 3 tbsp breadcrumbs
- 2 mushrooms thickly sliced
- 1 tbsp olive oil
- 1 chopped onion
- 1 tbsp chopped thyme
- 1 tsp salt
- Ground black pepper

Directions:

1 .Preheat air fryer to 200ºC
2 .Combine all the ingredients in a bowl
3 .Put the mix into a pan and press down firmly, coat with olive oil
4 .Place pan in the air fryer and cook for 25 minutes

Copycat Burger

Servings: 4

Ingredients:

- 400g minced pork
- 4 wholemeal burger buns
- Avocado sauce to taste
- 1 avocado
- 1 small onion, chopped
- 2 chopped spring onions
- Salad garnish
- 1 tbsp Worcester sauce
- 1 tbsp tomato ketchup
- 1 tsp garlic puree

1 tsp mixed herbs

Directions:

1 .In a bowl mix together the mince, onion, half the avocado and all of the seasoning
2 .Form into burgers
3 .Place in the air fryer and cook at 180ºC for 8 minutes
4 .When cooked place in the bun, layer with sauce and salad garnish

Mustard Glazed Pork

Servings: 4

Ingredients:

- 500g pork tenderloin
- 1 tbsp minced garlic
- ¼ tsp salt
- ⅛ tsp cracked black pepper
- 75g yellow mustard
- 3 tbsp brown sugar
- 1 tsp Italian seasoning
- 1 tsp rosemary

Directions:

1 .Cut slits into the pork place the minced garlic into the slits, season with the salt and pepper

2 .Add the remaining ingredients to a bowl and whisk to combine

3 .Rub the mix over the pork and allow to marinate for 2 hours

4 .Place in the air fryer and cook at 200ºC for 20 minutes

Traditional Pork Chops

Servings: 8

Ingredients:

- 8 pork chops
- 1 egg
- 100ml milk
- 300g bread crumbs
- 1 packet of dry ranch seasoning mix

Salt and pepper to taste

Directions:

1 .Preheat air fryer to 170ºC

2 .Beat the egg in a bowl, add the milk season with salt and pepper

3 .In another bowl mix the bread crumbs and ranch dressing mix

4 .Dip the pork into the egg then cover with breadcrumbs

Place in the air fryer and cook for 12 minutes turning half way

Pork Schnitzel

Servings: 2

Ingredients:

- 3 pork steaks, cut into cubes
- Salt and pepper
- 175g flour
- 2 eggs
- 175g breadcrumbs

Directions:

1 .Sprinkle the pork with salt and pepper
2 .Coat in the flour then dip in the egg
3 .Coat the pork in breadcrumbs
4 .Place in the air fryer and cook at 175ºC for 20 minutes turning halfway
5 .Serve with red cabbage

Beef Wellington

Servings: 4

Ingredients:

- 300g chicken liver pate
- 500g shortcrust pastry
- 600g beef fillet
- 1 egg beaten
- Salt and pepper

Directions:

1 .Remove all the visible fat from the beef season with salt and pepper. Wrap in cling film and place in the fridge for 1 hour
2 .Roll out the pastry, brush the edges with egg
3 .Spread the pate over the pastry. Remove the clingfilm from the beef and place in the center of the pastry
4 .Seal the pastry around the meat
5 .Place in the air fryer and cook at 160ºC for 35 minutes

Homemade Crispy Pepperoni Pizza

Servings: 4

Ingredients:

- For the pizza dough:
- 500 g / 17.6 oz plain flour
- 1 tsp salt
- 1 tsp dry non-fast-acting yeast
- 400 ml warm water
- For the toppings:
- 100 g / 3.5 oz tomato sauce
- 100 g / 3.5 oz mozzarella cheese, grated
- 8 slices pepperoni

Directions:

1 .To make the pizza dough, place the plain flour, salt, and dry yeast in a large mixing bowl. Pour in the warm water bit by bit until it forms a tacky dough.
2 .Lightly dust a clean kitchen top surface with plain flour and roll the dough out until it is around ½ an inch thick.
3 .Preheat your air fryer to 150 °C / 300 °F and line the bottom of the basket with parchment paper.
4 .Spread the tomato sauce evenly across the dough and top with grated mozzarella cheese. Top with the pepperoni slices and carefully transfer the pizza into the lined air fryer basket.
5 .Cook the pizza until the crust is golden and crispy, and the mozzarella cheese has melted.
6 .Enjoy the pizza while still hot with a side salad and some potato wedges.

Asparagus & Steak Parcels

Servings: 4

Ingredients:

- 500g flank steak, cut into 6 equal pieces
- 75ml Tamari sauce
- 2 crushed garlic cloves
- 250g trimmed asparagus
- 3 large bell peppers, thinly sliced
- 2 tbsp butter

Salt and pepper to taste

Directions:

1 .Season the steak to your liking
2 .Place the meat in a zip top bag and add the Tamari and garlic, sealing the bag closed
3 .Make sure the steaks are fully coated in the sauce and leave them in the fright at least 1 hour, but preferably overnight
4 .Remove the steaks from the bag and throw the marinade away
5 .Place the peppers and sliced asparagus in the centre of each steak piece
6 .Roll the steak up and secure in place with a tooth pick
7 .Preheat your air fryer to 250ºC
8 .Transfer the meat parcels to the air fryer and cook for 5 minutes
9 .Allow to rest before serving
10 .Melt the butter in a saucepan, over a medium heat, adding the juices from the air fryer
11 .Combine well and keep cooking until thickened
12 .Pour the sauce over the steak parcels and season to your liking

Steak Popcorn Bites

Servings: 4

Ingredients:

- 500g steak, cut into 1" sized cubes
- 500g potato chips, ridged ones work best
- 100g flour
- 2 beaten eggs
- Salt and pepper to taste

Directions:

1 .Place the chips into the food processor and pulse unit you get fine chip crumbs
2 .Take a bowl and combine the flour with salt and pepper
3 .Add the chips to another bowl and the beaten egg to another bowl
4 .Take the steak cubes and dip first in the flour, then the egg and then the chip crumbs
5 .Preheat your air fryer to 260ºC
6 .Place the steak pieces into the fryer and cook for 9 minutes

Hamburgers With Feta

Servings: 4

Ingredients:

- 400g minced beef
- 250g crumbled feta
- 25g chopped green olives
- ½ tsp garlic powder
- ½ cup chopped onion
- 2 tbsp Worcestershire sauce
- ½ tsp steak seasoning
- Salt to taste

Directions:

1 .Mix all the ingredients in a bowl
2 .Divide the mix into four and shape into patties
3 .Place in the air fryer and cook at 200ºC for about 15 minutes

Beef Stuffed Peppers

Servings: 4

Ingredients:

- 4 bell peppers
- ½ chopped onion
- 1 minced garlic clove
- 500g minced beef
- 5 tbsp tomato sauce
- 100g grated cheese
- 2 tsp Worcestershire sauce
- 1 tsp garlic powder
- A pinch of black pepper
- ½ tsp chilli powder
- 1 tsp dried basil
- 75g cooked rice

Directions:

1 .Cook the onions, minced beef, garlic and all the seasonings until the meat is browned

2 .Remove from the heat and add Worcestershire sauce, rice, ½ the cheese and ⅔ of the tomato sauce mix well

3 .Cut the tops off the peppers and remove the seeds

4 .Stuff the peppers with the mixture and place in the air fryer

5 .Cook at 200ºC for about 11 minutes

6 .When there are 3 minutes remaining top the peppers with the rest of the tomato sauce and cheese

Pork Belly With Crackling

Servings: 4

Ingredients:

- 800g belly pork
- 1 tsp sea salt
- 1 tsp garlic salt
- 2 tsp five spice
- 1 tsp rosemary
- 1 tsp white pepper
- 1 tsp sugar
- Half a lemon

Directions:

1 .Cut lines into the meat portion of the belly pork

2 .Cook thoroughly in water

3 .Allow to air dry for 3 hours

4 .Score the skin and prick holes with a fork

5 .Rub with the dry rub mix, rub some lemon juice on the skin

6 .Place in the air fryer and cook at 160ºC for 30 minutes then at 180ºC for a further 30 minutes

Chapter 4
Poultry Recipes

Bacon Wrapped Chicken Thighs

Servings: 4

Ingredients:

- 75g softened butter
- ½ clove minced garlic
- ¼ tsp dried thyme
- ¼ tsp dried basil
- ⅛ tsp coarse salt
- 100g thick cut bacon
- 350g chicken thighs, boneless and skinless
- 2 tsp minced garlic
- Salt and pepper to taste

Directions:

1 .Take a mixing bowl and add the softened butter, garlic, thyme, basil, salt and pepper, combining well
2 .Place the butter onto a sheet of plastic wrap and roll up to make a butter log
3 .Refrigerate for about 2 hours
4 .Remove the plastic wrap
5 .Place one bacon strip onto the butter and then place the chicken thighs on top of the bacon. Sprinkle with garlic
6 .Place the cold butter into the middle of the chicken thigh and tuck one end of bacon into the chicken
7 .Next, fold over the chicken thigh whilst rolling the bacon around
8 .Repeat with the rest
9 .Preheat the air fryer to 188C
10 .Cook the chicken until white in the centre and the juices run clear

Smoky Chicken Breast

Servings: 2

Ingredients:

- 2 halved chicken breasts
- 2 tsp olive oil
- 1 tsp ground thyme
- 2 tsp paprika
- 1tsp cumin
- 0.5 tsp cayenne pepper
- 0.5 tsp onion powder
- Salt and pepper to taste

Directions:

1 .In a medium bowl, combine the spices together
2 .Pour the spice mixture onto a plate
3 .Take each chicken breast and coat in the spices, pressing down to ensure an even distribution
4 .Place the chicken to one side for 5 minutes
5 .Preheat your air fryer to 180ºC
6 .Arrange the chicken inside the fryer and cook for 10 minutes
7 .Turn the chicken over and cook for another 10 minutes
8 .Remove from the fryer and allow to sit for 5 minutes before serving

Charred Chicken Breasts

Servings: 2

Ingredients:

- 2 tsp paprika
- 1 tsp ground thyme
- 1 tsp cumin
- ½ tsp cayenne pepper
- ½ tsp onion powder
- ½ tsp black pepper
- ¼ tsp salt
- 2 tsp vegetable oil
- 2 skinless boneless chicken breasts, cut into halves

Directions:

1 .Take a bowl and add the paprika, thyme, cumin, cayenne pepper, onion powder, black pepper and salt
2 .Coat each chicken breast with oil and dredge chicken in the spice mixture
3 .Preheat air fryer to 175C
4 .Cook for 10 minutes and flip
5 .Cook for 10 more minutes

Pizza Chicken Nuggets

Servings: 2

Ingredients:

- 60 g/¾ cup dried breadcrumbs (see page 9)
- 20 g/¼ cup grated Parmesan
- ½ teaspoon dried oregano
- ¼ teaspoon freshly ground black pepper
- 150 g/⅔ cup Mediterranean sauce (see page 102) or 150 g/5½ oz. jarred tomato pasta sauce (keep any leftover sauce for serving)
- 400 g/14 oz. chicken fillets

Directions:

1 .Preheat the air-fryer to 180ºC/350ºF.

2 .Combine the breadcrumbs, Parmesan, oregano and pepper in a bowl. Have the Mediterranean or pasta sauce in a separate bowl.

3 .Dip each chicken fillet in the tomato sauce first, then roll in the breadcrumb mix until coated fully.

4 .Add the breaded fillets to the preheated air-fryer and air-fry for 10 minutes. Check the internal temperature of the chicken has reached at least 74ºC/165ºF using a meat thermometer – if not, cook for another few minutes.

5 .Serve with some additional sauce that has been warmed through.

Whole Chicken

Servings: 4

Ingredients:

- 1.5-kg/3¼-lb. chicken
- 2 tablespoons butter or coconut oil
- salt and freshly ground black pepper

Directions:

1 .Place the chicken breast-side up and carefully insert the butter or oil between the skin and the flesh of each breast. Season.

2 .Preheat the air-fryer to 180ºC/350ºF. If the chicken hits the heating element, remove the drawer to lower the chicken a level.

3 .Add the chicken to the preheated air-fryer breast-side up. Air-fry for 30 minutes, then turn over and cook for a further 10 minutes. Check the internal temperature with a meat thermometer. If it is 75ºC/167ºF at the thickest part, remove the chicken from the air-fryer and leave to rest for 10 minutes before carving. If less than 75ºC/167ºF, continue to cook until this internal temperature is reached and then allow to rest.

Turkey Cutlets In Mushroom Sauce

Servings: 2

Ingredients:

- 2 turkey cutlets
- 1 tbsp butter
- 1 can of cream of mushroom sauce
- 160ml milk

Salt and pepper for seasoning

Directions:

1 .Preheat the air fryer to 220ºC

2 .Brush the turkey cults with the butter and seasoning

3 .Place in the air fryer and cook for 11 minutes

4 .Add the mushroom soup and milk to a pan and cook over the stone for around 10 minutes, stirring every so often

5 .Top the turkey cutlets with the sauce

Chicken Kiev

Servings: 4

Ingredients:

- 4 boneless chicken breasts
- 4 tablespoons plain/all-purpose flour (gluten-free if you wish)
- 1 egg, beaten
- 130 g/2 cups dried breadcrumbs (gluten-free if you wish, see page 9)
- GARLIC BUTTER
- 60 g/4 tablespoons salted butter, softened
- 1 large garlic clove, finely chopped

Directions:

1 .Mash together the butter and garlic. Form into a sausage shape, then slice into 4 equal discs. Place in the freezer until frozen.

2 .Make a deep horizontal slit across each chicken breast, taking care not to cut through to the other side. Stuff the cavity with a disc of frozen garlic butter. Place the flour in a shallow bowl, the egg in another and the breadcrumbs in a third. Coat each chicken breast first in flour, then egg, then breadcrumbs.

3 .Preheat the air-fryer to 180ºC/350ºF.

4 .Add the chicken Kievs to the preheated air-fryer and air-fry for 12 minutes until cooked through. This is hard to gauge as the butter inside the breast is not an indicator of doneness, so test the meat in the centre with a meat thermometer – it should be at least 75ºC/167ºF; if not, cook for another few minutes.

Crunchy Chicken Tenders

Servings: 4

Ingredients:

- 8 regular chicken tenders (frozen work best)
- 1 egg
- 2 tbsp olive oil
- 150g dried breadcrumbs

Directions:

1 .Heat the fryer to 175ºC
2 .In a small bowl, beat the egg
3 .In another bowl, combine the oil and the breadcrumbs together
4 .Take one tender and first dip it into the egg, and then cover it in the breadcrumb mixture
5 .Place the tender into the fryer basket
f.Repeat with the rest of the tenders, arranging them carefully so they don't touch inside the basket
6 .Cook for 12 minutes, checking that they are white in the centre before serving

Chicken Balls, Greek-style

Servings: 4

Ingredients:

- 500g ground chicken
- 1 egg
- 1 tbsp dried oregano
- 1.5 tbsp garlic paste
- 1 tsp lemon zest
- 1 tsp dried onion powder
- Salt and pepper to taste

Directions:

1 .Take a bowl and combine all ingredients well
2 .Use your hands to create meatballs - you should be able to make 12 balls
3 .Preheat your air fryer to 260ºC
4 .Add the meatballs to the fryer and cook for 9 minutes

Air Fried Maple Chicken Thighs

Servings: 4

Ingredients:

- 200ml buttermilk
- ½ tbsp maple syrup
- 1 egg
- 1 tsp granulated garlic salt
- 4 chicken thighs with the bone in
- 140g all purpose flour
- 65g tapioca flour
- 1 tsp sweet paprika
- 1 tsp onion powder
- ¼ tsp ground black pepper
- ¼ tsp cayenne pepper
- ½ tsp granulated garlic
- ½ tsp honey powder

Directions:

1 .Take a bowl and combine the buttermilk, maple syrup, egg and garlic powder
2 .Transfer to a bag and add chicken thighs, shaking to combine well
3 .Set aside for 1 hour
4 .Take a shallow bowl and add the flour, tapioca flour, salt, sweet paprika, smoked paprika, pepper, cayenne pepper and honey powder, combining well
5 .Preheat the air fryer to 190ºC
6 .Drag the chicken through flour mixture and place the chicken skin side down in the air fryer Cook for 12 minutes, until white in the middle

Chicken Tikka

Servings: 2

Ingredients:

- 2 chicken breasts, diced
- FIRST MARINADE
- freshly squeezed juice of ½ a lemon
- 1 tablespoon freshly grated ginger
- 1 tablespoon freshly grated garlic
- a good pinch of salt
- SECOND MARINADE
- 100 g/½ cup Greek yogurt
- ½ teaspoon chilli powder
- ½ teaspoon chilli paste
- ½ teaspoon turmeric
- ½ teaspoon garam masala
- 1 tablespoon olive oil

Directions:

1 .Mix the ingredients for the first marinade together in a bowl, add in the chicken and stir to coat all the chicken pieces. Leave in the fridge to marinate for 20 minutes.
2 .Combine the second marinade ingredients. Once the first marinade has had 20 minutes, add the second marinade to the chicken and stir well. Leave in the fridge for at least 4 hours.
3 .Preheat the air-fryer to 180ºC/350ºF.
4 .Thread the chicken pieces onto metal skewers that fit in your air-fryer. Add the skewers to the preheated air-fryer and air-fry for 10 minutes. Check the internal temperature of the chicken has reached at least 74ºC/165ºF using a meat thermometer – if not, cook for another few minutes and then serve.

Chicken And Cheese Chimichangas

Servings: 6

Ingredients:

- 100g shredded chicken (cooked)
- 150g nacho cheese
- 1 chopped jalapeño pepper
- 6 flour tortillas
- 5 tbsp salsa
- 60g refried beans
- 1 tsp cumin
- 0.5 tsp chill powder
- Salt and pepper to taste

Directions:

1 .Take a large mixing bowl and add all of the ingredients, combining well
2 .Add ⅓ of the filling to each tortilla and roll into a burrito shape
3 .Spray the air fryer with cooking spray and heat to 200ºC
4 .Place the chimichangas in the air fryer and cook for 7 minutes

Chicken Tikka Masala

Servings: 4

Ingredients:

- 100g tikka masala curry pasta
- 200g low fat yogurt
- 600g skinless chicken breasts
- 1 tbsp vegetable oil
- 1 onion, chopped
- 400g can of the whole, peeled tomatoes
- 20ml water
- 1 tbsp sugar
- 2 tbsp lemon juice
- 1 small bunch of chopped coriander leaves

Directions:

1 .Take a bowl and combine the tikka masala curry paste with half the yogurt
2 .Cut the chicken into strips
3 .Preheat the air fryer to 200ºC
4 .Add the yogurt mixture and coat the chicken until fully covered
5 .Place into the refrigerator for 2 hours
6 .Place the oil and onion in the air fryer and cook for 10 minutes
7 .Add the marinated chicken, tomatoes, water and the rest of the yogurt and combine
8 .Add the sugar and lemon juice and combine again
9 .Cook for 15 minutes

Grain-free Chicken Katsu

Servings: 4

Ingredients:

- 125 g/1¼ cups ground almonds
- ½ teaspoon salt
- ½ teaspoon garlic powder
- ½ teaspoon dried parsley
- ½ teaspoon freshly ground black pepper
- ¼ teaspoon onion powder
- ¼ teaspoon dried oregano
- 450 g/1 lb. mini chicken fillets
- 1 egg, beaten
- oil, for spraying/drizzling
- coriander/cilantro leaves, to serve
- KATSU SAUCE
- 1 teaspoon olive oil or avocado oil
- 1 courgette/zucchini (approx. 150 g/5 oz.), finely chopped
- 1 carrot (approx. 100 g/3½ oz.), finely chopped
- 1 onion (approx. 120 g/4½ oz.), finely chopped
- 1 eating apple (approx. 150 g/5 oz.), cored and finely chopped
- 1 teaspoon ground ginger
- 1 teaspoon ground turmeric
- 2 teaspoons ground cumin
- 2 teaspoons ground coriander
- 1½ teaspoons mild chilli/chili powder
- 1 teaspoon garlic powder
- 1½ tablespoons runny honey
- 1 tablespoon soy sauce (gluten-free if you wish)

700 ml/3 cups vegetable stock (700 ml/3 cups water with 1½ stock cubes)

Directions:

1 .First make the sauce. The easiest way to ensure all the vegetables and apple are finely chopped is to combine them in a food processor. Heat the oil in a large saucepan and sauté the finely chopped vegetables and apple for 5 minutes. Add all the seasonings, honey, soy sauce and stock and stir well, then bring to a simmer and simmer for 30 minutes.

2 .Meanwhile, mix together the ground almonds, seasonings and spices. Dip each chicken fillet into the beaten egg, then into the almond-spice mix, making sure each fillet is fully coated. Spray the coated chicken fillets with olive oil (or simply drizzle over).

3 .Preheat the air-fryer to 180ºC/350ºF.

4 .Place the chicken fillets in the preheated air-fryer and air-fry for 10 minutes, turning halfway through cooking. Check the internal temperature of the chicken has reached at least 74ºC/165ºF using a meat thermometer – if not, cook for another few minutes.

5 .Blend the cooked sauce in a food processor until smooth. Serve the chicken with the Katsu Sauce drizzled over (if necessary, reheat the sauce gently before serving) and scattered with coriander leaves. Any unused sauce can be frozen.

Sticky Chicken Tikka Drumsticks

Servings: 4

Ingredients:

- 12 chicken drumsticks
- MARINADE
- 100 g/½ cup Greek yogurt
- 2 tablespoons tikka paste
- 2 teaspoons ginger preserve
- freshly squeezed juice of ½ a lemon
- ¾ teaspoon salt

Directions:

1 .Make slices across each of the drumsticks with a sharp knife. Mix the marinade ingredients together in a bowl, then add the drumsticks. Massage the marinade into the drumsticks, then leave to marinate in the fridge overnight or for at least 6 hours.

2 .Preheat the air-fryer to 200ºC/400ºF.

3 .Lay the drumsticks on an air-fryer liner or a piece of pierced parchment paper. Place the paper and drumsticks in the preheated air-fryer. Air-fry for 6 minutes, then turn over and cook for a further 6 minutes. Check the internal temperature of the drumsticks has reached at least 75ºC/167ºF using a meat thermometer – if not, cook for another few minutes and then serve.

Hawaiian Chicken

Servings: 2

Ingredients:

- 2 chicken breasts
- 1 tbsp butter
- A pinch of salt and pepper
- 160ml pineapple juice
- 25g brown sugar
- 3 tbsp soy sauce
- 2 tsp water
- 1 clove of garlic, minced
- 1 tsp grated ginger
- 2 tsp cornstarch

Directions:

1 .Preheat the air fryer to 260ºC

2 .Take a bowl and combine the butter and salt and pepper

3 .Cover the chicken with the butter and cook in the fryer for 15 minutes, turning halfway

4 .Remove and allow to rest for 5 minutes

5 .Take another bowl and mix together the pineapple juice, soy sauce, garlic, ginger, and brown sugar

6 .Transfer to a saucepan and simmer for 5 minutes

7 .Combine the water and cornstarch and add to the sauce, stirring continually for another minute

8 .Slice the chicken into strips and pour the sauce over the top

Nashville Chicken

Servings: 4

Ingredients:

- 400g boneless chicken breast tenders
- 2 tsp salt
- 2 tsp coarsely ground black pepper
- 2 tbsp hot sauce
- 2 tbsp pickle juice
- 500g all purpose flour
- 3 large eggs
- 300ml buttermilk
- 2 tbsp olive oil
- 6 tbsp cayenne pepper
- 3 tbsp dark brown sugar
- 1 tsp chilli powder
- 1 tsp garlic powder
- 1 tsp paprika
- Salt and pepper to taste

Directions:

1 .Take a large mixing bowl and add the chicken, hot sauce, pickle juice, salt and pepper and combine
2 .Place in the refrigerator for 3 hours
3 .Transfer the flour to a bowl
4 .Take another bowl and add the eggs, buttermilk and 1 tbsp of the hot sauce, combining well
5 .Press each piece of chicken into the flour and coat well
6 .Place the chicken into the buttermilk mixture and then back into the flour
7 .Allow to sit or 10 minutes
8 .Preheat the air fryer to 193C
9 .Whisk together the spices, brown sugar and olive oil to make the sauce and pour over the chicken tenders
10 .Serve whilst still warm

Chapter 5 Fish & Seafood Recipes

Chilli Lime Tilapia

Servings: 3

Ingredients:

- 500g Tilapia fillets
- 25g panko crumbs
- 200g flour
- Salt and pepper to taste
- 2 eggs
- 1 tbsp chilli powder
- The juice of 1 lime

Directions:

1 .Mix panko, salt and pepper and chilli powder together
2 .Whisk the egg in a separate bowl
3 .Spray the air fryer with cooking spray
4 .Dip the tilapia in the flour, then in the egg and cover in the panko mix
5 .Place fish in the air fryer, spray with cooking spray and cook for 7-8 minutes at 190ºC
6 .Turn the fish over and cook for a further 7-8 minutes until golden brown.
7 .Squeeze lime juice over the top and serve

Garlic-parsley Prawns

Servings: 2

Ingredients:

- 300 g/10½ oz. raw king prawns/jumbo shrimp (without shell)
- 40 g/3 tablespoons garlic butter, softened (see page 72)
- 2 tablespoons freshly chopped flat-leaf parsley

Directions:

1 .Thread the prawns/shrimp onto 6 metal skewers that will fit your air-fryer. Mix together the softened garlic butter and parsley and brush evenly onto the prawn skewers.
2 .Preheat the air-fryer to 180ºC/350ºF.
3 .Place the skewers on an air-fryer liner or a piece of pierced parchment paper. Add the skewers to the preheated air-fryer and air-fry for 2 minutes, then turn the skewers over and cook for a further 2 minutes. Check the internal temperature of the prawns has reached at least 50ºC/120ºF using a meat thermometer – if not, cook for another few minutes and serve.

Crunchy Fish

Servings: 4

Ingredients:

- 200g dry breadcrumbs
- 4 tbsp olive oil
- 4 fillets of white fish
- 1 beaten egg
- 1 sliced lemon

Directions:

1 .Heat the fryer to 180ºC
2 .In a medium mixing bowl, combine the olive oil and the breadcrumbs
3 .Take the fish and first dip it into the egg and then the breadcrumbs, making sure they are evenly coated well
4 .Arrange the fish into the basket
5 .Cook for 12 minutes
6 .Remove and serve with lemon slices

Air Fryer Tuna

Servings: 2

Ingredients:

- 2 tuna steaks, boneless and skinless
- 2 tsp honey
- 1 tsp grated ginger
- 4 tbsp soy sauce
- 1 tsp sesame oil
- 1/2 tsp rice vinegar

Directions:

1 .Combine the honey, soy sauce, rice vinegar and sesame oil in a bowl until totally mixed together
2 .Cover the tuna steaks with the sauce and place in the refrigerator for half an hour to marinade
3 .Preheat the air fryer to 270ºC
4 .Cook the tuna for 4 minutes
5 .Allow to rest before slicing

Mahi Fish Tacos

Servings: 4

Ingredients:

- 400g fresh mahi
- 8 small corn tortillas
- 2 tsp cajun seasoning
- 5 tbsp sour cream
- 2 tbsp mayonnaise
- 2 tbsp scotch bonnet pepper sauce (use 1 tbsp if you don't like your food too spicy)
- 1 tbsp sriracha sauce
- 2 tbsp lime juice
- Salt and pepper to taste
- 1 tbsp vegetable oil

Directions:

1 .Clean the mahi. Cut into half inch slices and season with salt
2 .Mix quarter parts cayenne pepper and black pepper with cajun seasoning. Sprinkle onto fish
3 .Brush pepper sauce on both sides of the fish
4 .Set the air fryer to 180ºC and cook for about 10 minutes or until golden brown
5 .Whilst the fish cooks make the chipotle lime cream. Mix the mayo, sour cream, lime juice sriracha and cayenne pepper
6 .Assemble tacos and enjoy

Salt & Pepper Calamari

Servings: 2

Ingredients:

- 500g squid rings
- 500g panko breadcrumbs
- 250g plain flour
- 2 tbsp pepper
- 2 tbsp salt
- 200ml buttermilk
- 1 egg

Directions:

1 .Take a medium bowl and combine the buttermilk and egg, stirring well
2 .Take another bowl and combine the salt, pepper, flour, and panko breadcrumbs, combining again
3 .Dip the quid into the buttermilk first and then the breadcrumbs, coating evenly
4 .Place in the air fryer basket
5 .Cook at 150ºC for 12 minutes, until golden

Honey Sriracha Salmon

Servings: 2

Ingredients:

- 25g sriracha
- 25g honey
- 500g salmon fillets
- 1 tbsp soy sauce

Directions:

1 .Mix the honey, soy sauce and sriracha, keep half the mix to one side for dipping
2 .Place the salmon in the sauce skin side up and marinade for 30 minutes
3 .Spray air fryer basket with cooking spray
4 .Heat the air fryer to 200ºC
5 .Place salmon in the air fryer skin side down and cook for 12 minutes

Ranch Style Fish Fillets

Servings: 4

Ingredients:

- 200g bread crumbs
- 30g ranch-style dressing mix
- 2 tbsp oil
- 2 beaten eggs
- 4 fish fillets of your choice
- Lemon wedges to garnish

Directions:

1 .Preheat air fryer to 180ºC
2 .Mix the bread crumbs and ranch dressing mix together, add in the oil until the mix becomes crumbly
3 .Dip the fish into the, then cover in the breadcrumb mix
4 .Place in the air fryer and cook for 12-13 minutes

Copycat Fish Fingers

Servings: 2

Ingredients:

- 2 slices wholemeal bread, grated into breadcrumbs
- 50g plain flour
- 1 beaten egg
- 1 white fish fillet
- The juice of 1 small lemon
- 1 tsp parsley
- 1 tsp thyme
- 1 tsp mixed herbs
- Salt and pepper to taste

Directions:

1 .Preheat the air fryer to 180ºC
2 .Add salt pepper and parsley to the breadcrumbs and combine well
3 .Place the egg in another bowl
4 .Place the flour in a separate bowl
5 .Place the fish into a food processor and add the lemon juice, salt, pepper thyme and mixed herbs
6 .Blitz to create a crumb-like consistency
7 .Roll your fish in the flour, then the egg and then the breadcrumbs
8 .Cook at 180ºC for 8 minutes

Baked Panko Cod

Servings: 5

Ingredients:

- 400g cod, cut into 5 pieces
- 250g panko breadcrumbs
- 1 egg plus 1 egg white extra
- Cooking spray
- ½ tsp onion powder
- ½ tsp garlic salt
- ⅛ tsp black pepper
- ½ tsp mixed herbs

Directions:

1 .Heat air fryer to 220ºC
2 .Beat the egg and egg white in a bowl
3 .Sprinkle fish with herbs and spice mix, dip into the egg and then cover in the panko bread crumbs
4 .Line air fryer basket with tin foil. Place the fish in the air fryer and coat with cooking spray
5 .Cook for about 15 minutes until, fish is lightly browned

Cajun Prawn Skewers

Servings: 2

Ingredients:

- 350 g/12 oz. king prawns/jumbo shrimp
- MARINADE
- 1 teaspoon smoked paprika
- 1 teaspoon unrefined sugar
- 1 teaspoon salt
- ½ teaspoon onion powder
- ½ teaspoon mustard powder
- ¼ teaspoon dried oregano
- ¼ teaspoon dried thyme
- 1 teaspoon white wine vinegar
- 2 teaspoons olive oil

Directions:

1 .Mix all the marinade ingredients together in a bowl. Mix the prawns/shrimp into the marinade and cover. Place in the fridge to marinate for at least an hour.
2 .Preheat the air-fryer to 180ºC/350ºF.
3 .Thread 4–5 prawns/shrimp on to each skewer (you should have enough for 4–5 skewers). Add the skewers to the preheated air-fryer and air-fry for 2 minutes, then turn the skewers and cook for a further 2 minutes. Check the internal temperature of the prawns/shrimp has reached at least 50ºC/125ºF using a meat thermometer – if not, cook for another few minutes. Serve immediately.

Mushrooms Stuffed With Crab

Servings: 2

Ingredients:

- 500g large mushrooms
- 2 tsp salt
- Half a diced red onion
- 2 diced celery sticks
- 300g lump crab
- 35g seasoned breadcrumbs
- 1 egg
- 1 tsp oregano
- 1 tsp hot sauce
- 50g grated Parmesan cheese

Directions:

1 .Preheat to 260ºC
2 .Take a baking sheet and arrange the mushrooms top down
3 .Spray with a little cooking oil
4 .Take a bowl and combine the onions, celery, breadcrumbs, egg, crab and half the cheese, oregano and hot sauce
5 .Fill each mushroom with the mixture and make sure it's heaped over the top
6 .Cover with the rest of the cheese
7 .Place in the air fryer for 18 minutes

Garlic Tilapia

Servings: 2

Ingredients:

- 2 tilapia fillets
- 2 tsp chopped fresh chives
- 2 tsp chopped fresh parsley
- 2 tsp olive oil
- 1 tsp minced garlic
- Salt and pepper for seasoning

Directions:

1 .Preheat the air fryer to 220ºC
2 .Take a small bowl and combine the olive oil with the chives, garlic, parsley and a little salt and pepper
3 .Brush the mixture over the fish fillets
4 .Place the fish into the air fryer and cook for 10 minutes, until flaky

Garlic Butter Salmon

Servings: 2

Ingredients:

- 2 salmon fillets, boneless with the skin left on
- 1 tsp minced garlic
- 2 tbsp melted butter
- 1 tsp chopped parsley
- Salt and pepper to taste

Directions:

1 .Preheat the air fryer to 270 °C
2 .Take a bowl and combine the melted butter, parsley and garlic to create a sauce
3 .Season the salmon to your liking
4 .Brush the salmon with the garlic mixture, on both sides
5 .Place the salmon into the fryer, with the skin side facing down
6 .Cook for 10 minutes - the salmon is done when it flakes with ease

Crispy Nacho Prawns

Servings: 6

Ingredients:

- 1 egg
- 18 large prawns
- 1 bag of nacho cheese flavoured corn chips, crushed

Directions:

1 .Wash the prawns and pat dry
2 .Place the chips into a bowl
3 .In another bowl, whisk the egg
4 .Dip the prawns into the egg and then the nachos
5 .Preheat the air fryer to 180°C
6 .Cook for 8 minutes

Tandoori Salmon

Servings: 4

Ingredients:

- 300g salmon
- 1 tbsp butter
- 1 tbsp tandoori spice
- Salt and pepper to taste
- 1 small tomato
- Half a red onion
- 600g plain yogurt
- 30 fresh mint leaves, chopped
- 1 tsp minced green chilli
- 1 tbsp ground cumin
- Half a cucumber, chopped

Directions:

1 .Cut the salmon into cubes and coat in the tandoori spice mix. Chill for 30 minutes to marinate

2 .Blend mint, cumin and chilli with ¼ of the yogurt refrigerate and leave to steep

3 .Peel the tomato and cut into cubes. Peel the cucumber and chop into cubes, finely dice the onion

4 .Cook the salmon in the air fryer for 5-6 minutes at 200ºC

5 .Mix the flavoured yogurt with the remaining yogurt, tomato, cucumber and onion

6 .Place the sauce in serving bowls and place the salmon on top

Zesty Fish Fillets

Servings: 2

Ingredients:

- 30g dry ranch seasoning
- 2 beaten eggs
- 100g breadcrumbs
- 2.5 tbsp vegetable oil
- 4 fish fillets of your choice
- Wedges of lemon to serve

Directions:

1 .Preheat the air fryer to 180ºC

2 .Mix the bread crumbs and seasoning together add the oil and combine

3 .Dip the fish into the egg and then coat in the breadcrumb mix

4 .Place in the air fryer and cook for 12 minutes

5 .Serve with lemon wedges

Chapter 6 Vegetarian & Vegan Recipes

Macaroni & Cheese Quiche

Servings: 4

Ingredients:

- 8 tbsp macaroni pasta
- 1 block of short crust pastry
- 2 tbsp Greek yogurt
- 2 eggs
- 150ml milk
- 1 tsp garlic puree
- 400g grated cheese

Directions:

1 .Rub the inside of 4 ramekins with flour
2 .Line the ramekins with the pastry
3 .Mix the yogurt, garlic and macaroni. Add to the ramekins until ¾ full
4 .Mix the egg and milk together and pour over the macaroni. Sprinkle with cheese
5 .Heat the air fryer to 180ºC and cook for 20 minutes until golden brown.

Roasted Cauliflower

Servings: 2

Ingredients:

- 3 cloves garlic
- 1 tbsp peanut oil
- ½ tsp salt
- ½ tsp paprika
- 400g cauliflower florets

Directions:

1 .Preheat air fryer to 200ºC
2 .Crush the garlic, place all ingredients in bowl and mix well
3 .Place in the air fryer and cook for about 15 minutes, shaking every 5 minutes

Spinach And Egg Air Fryer Breakfast Muffins

Servings: 4

Ingredients:

- 8 eggs
- 100 g / 3.5 oz fresh spinach
- 50 g / 1.8 oz cheddar cheese, grated
- ½ onion, finely sliced
- 1 tsp black pepper

Directions:

1 .Preheat your air fryer to 200 °C / 400 °F and line an 8-pan muffin tray with parchment paper or grease with olive oil.
2 .Gently press the spinach leaves into the bottom of each prepared muffin cup.
3 .Sprinkle the finely sliced onion on top of the spinach.
4 .Crack 2 eggs into each cup on top of the spinach and add some of the grated cheddar cheese on top of the eggs. Top with a light sprinkle of black pepper.
5 .Carefully place the muffins into the air fryer basket and shut the lid. Bake for 10 minutes until the eggs are set and the muffins are hot throughout.
6 .Serve the muffins while still hot for breakfast.

Courgette Burgers

Servings: 4

Ingredients:

- 1 courgette
- 1 small can of chickpeas, drained
- 3 spring onions
- Pinch of dried garlic
- Salt and pepper
- 3 tbsp coriander
- 1 tsp chilli powder
- 1 tsp mixed spice
- 1 tsp cumin

Directions:

1 .Grate the courgette and drain the excess water
2 .Thinly slice the spring onions and add to the bowl with the chickpeas, courgette and seasoning
3 .Bind the ingredients and form into patties
4 .Place in the air fryer and cook for 12 minutes at 200ºC

Ravioli Air Fryer Style

Servings: 4

Ingredients:

- Half a pack of frozen ravioli
- 200g Italian breadcrumbs
- 200ml buttermilk
- 5 tbsp marinara sauce
- 1 tbsp olive oil

Directions:

1. Preheat the air fryer to 220ºC
2. Place the buttermilk in a bowl
3. Add the breadcrumbs to another bowl
4. Take each piece of ravioli and dip it first into the buttermilk and then into the breadcrumbs, coating evenly
5. Add the ravioli to the air fryer and cook for 7 minutes, adding a small amount of oil at the halfway point
6. Serve with the marinara sauce on the side

Chickpea And Sweetcorn Falafel

Servings: 4

Ingredients:

- ½ onion, sliced
- 2 cloves garlic, peeled and sliced
- 2 tbsp fresh parsley, chopped
- 2 tbsp fresh coriander, chopped
- 2 x 400 g / 14 oz chickpeas, drained and rinsed
- 1 tsp salt
- 1 tsp black pepper
- 1 tsp baking powder
- 1 tsp dried mixed herbs
- 1 tsp cumin
- 1 tsp chili powder
- 50 g / 1.8 oz sweetcorn, fresh or frozen

Directions:

1 .Preheat the air fryer to 180 °C / 350 °F and line the bottom of the basket with parchment paper.
2 .In a food processor, place the onion, garlic cloves, fresh parsley, and fresh coriander. Pulse the ingredients in 30-second intervals until they form a smooth mixture. Scrape the mixture from the sides of the food processor in between each interval if necessary.
3 .Mix in the chickpeas, salt, black pepper, baking powder, dried mixed herbs, cumin, and chili powder. Pulse the mixture until fully combined and smooth. Add more water if the mixture is looking a bit dry. The mixture should be dry but not crumbly.
4 .Use a spoon to scoop out 2 tbsp of the chickpea mixture at a time and roll into small, even falafels.
5 .Transfer the falafels into the prepared air fryer basket and cook for 12-15 minutes.
6 .Serve the falafels either hot or cold as a side dish to your main meal or as part of a large salad.

Camembert & Soldiers

Servings: 2

Ingredients:

- 1 piece of Camembert
- 2 slices sandwich bread
- 1 tbsp mustard

Directions:

1. Preheat the air fryer to 180ºC
2. Place the camembert in a sturdy container, cook in the air fryer for 15 minutes
3. Toast the bread and cut into soldiers
4. Serve with the mustard by the side

Onion Dumplings

Servings: 2

Ingredients:

- 14 frozen dumplings (pierogies)
- 1 onion
- 1 tbsp olive oil
- 1 tsp sugar

Directions:

1. Take a large saucepan and fill with water, bringing to the boil
2. Cook the dumplings for 5 minutes, remove and drain
3. Slice the onion into long pieces
4. Oil the air fryer basket and preheat to 220ºC
5. Cook the onion for 12 minutes, stirring often. After 5 minutes, add the sugar and combine
6. Remove the onions and place to one side
7. Add the dumplings to the air fryer and cook for 4 minutes
8. Turn the temperature up to 270ºC and cook for another 3 minutes
9. Mix the dumplings with the onions before serving

Air Fryer Cheese Sandwich

Servings: 2

Ingredients:

- 4 slices white or wholemeal bread
- 2 tbsp butter
- 50 g / 3.5 oz cheddar cheese, grated

Directions:

1 .Preheat the air fryer to 180 °C / 350 °F and line the bottom of the basket with parchment paper.
2 .Lay the slices of bread out on a clean surface and butter one side of each. Evenly sprinkle the cheese on two of the slices and cover with the final two slices.
3 .Transfer the sandwiches to the air fryer, close the lid, and cook for 5 minutes until the bread is crispy and golden, and the cheese is melted.

Flat Mushroom Pizzas

Servings: 1

Ingredients:

- 2 portobello mushrooms, cleaned and stalk removed
- 6 mozzarella balls
- 1 teaspoon olive oil
- PIZZA SAUCE
- 100 g/3½ oz. passata/ strained tomatoes
- 1 teaspoon dried oregano
- ¼ teaspoon garlic salt

Directions:

1 .Preheat the air-fryer to 180ºC/350ºF.
2 .Mix the ingredients for the pizza sauce together in a small bowl. Fill each upturned portobello mushroom with sauce, then top each with three mozzarella balls and drizzle the olive oil over.
3 .Add the mushrooms to the preheated air-fryer and air-fry for 8 minutes. Serve immediately.

Pakoras

Servings: 8

Ingredients:

- 200g chopped cauliflower
- 100g diced pepper
- 250g chickpea flour
- 30ml water
- ½ tsp cumin
- Cooking spray
- 1 onion, diced
- 1 tsp salt
- 1 garlic clove, minced
- 1 tsp curry powder
- 1 tsp coriander
- ½ tsp cayenne

Directions:

1 .Preheat air fryer to 175ºC
2 .Place all ingredients in a bowl and mix well
3 .Spray cooking basket with oil
4 .Spoon 2 tbsp of mix into the basket and flatten, continue until the basket is full
5 .Cook for 8 minutes, turn then cook for a further 8 minutes

Roast Cauliflower & Broccoli

Servings: 4

Ingredients:

- 300g broccoli
- 300g cauliflower
- 2 tbsp oil
- ½ tsp garlic powder
- ¼ tsp salt
- ¼ tsp paprika
- ⅛ tsp pepper

Directions:

1 .Preheat air fryer to 200ºC
2 .Place broccoli and cauliflower in a bowl and microwave for 3 minutes
3 .Add remaining ingredients and mix well
4 .Add to the air fryer and cook for about 12 mins

Lentil Burgers

Servings: 4

Ingredients:

- 100g black buluga lentils
- 1 carrot, grated
- 1 diced onion
- 100g white cabbage
- 300g oats
- 1 tbsp garlic puree
- 1 tsp cumin
- Salt and pepper

Directions:

1 .Blend the oats until they resemble flour
2 .Put the lentils in a pan with water and cook for 45 minutes
3 .Steam your vegetables for 5 minutes
4 .Add all the ingredients into a bowl and mix well to combine
5 .Form into burgers place in the air fryer and cook at 180ºC for 30 minutes

Broccoli Cheese

Servings: 2

Ingredients:

- 250g broccoli
- Cooking spray
- 10 tbsp evaporated milk
- 300g Mexican cheese
- 4 tsp Amarillo paste
- 6 saltine crackers

Directions:

1 .Heat the air fryer to 190ºC
2 .Place the broccoli in the air fryer spray with cooking oil and cook for about 6 minutes
3 .Place the remaining ingredients in a blender and process until smooth
4 .Place in a bowl and microwave for 30 seconds
5 .Pour over the broccoli and serve

Ratatouille

Servings: 4

Ingredients:

- ½ small aubergine, cubed
- 1 courgette, cubed
- 1 tomato, cubed
- 1 pepper, cut into cubes
- ½ onion, diced
- 1 fresh cayenne pepper, sliced
- 1 tsp vinegar
- 5 sprigs basil, chopped
- 2 sprigs oregano, chopped
- 1 clove garlic, crushed
- Salt and pepper
- 1 tbsp olive oil
- 1 tbsp white wine

Directions:

1 .Preheat air fryer to 200ºC
2 .Place all ingredients in a bowl and mix
3 .Pour into a baking dish
4 .Add dish to the air fryer and cook for 8 minutes, stir then cook for another 10 minutes

Roast Vegetables

Servings: 4

Ingredients:

- 100g diced courgette
- 100g diced squash
- 100g diced mushrooms
- 100g diced cauliflower
- 100g diced asparagus
- 100g diced pepper
- 2 tsp oil
- ½ tsp salt
- ¼ tsp pepper
- ¼ tsp seasoning

Directions:

1 .Preheat air fryer to 180ºC
2 .Mix all ingredients together
3 .Add to air fryer and cook for 10 minutes stirring halfway

Chapter 7 Desserts Recipes

Key Lime Cupcakes

Servings: 6

Ingredients:

- 250g Greek yogurt
- 200g soft cheese
- 2 eggs
- Juice and rind of 2 limes
- 1 egg yolk
- ¼ cup caster sugar
- 1 tsp vanilla essence

Directions:

1 .Mix the Greek yogurt and soft cheese together until smooth
2 .Add the eggs and mix, add the lime juice, rind, vanilla and caster sugar and mix well
3 .Fill 6 cupcake cases with the mix and place the rest to one side
4 .Place in the air fryer and cook at 160ºC for 10 minutes then another 10 minutes at 180ºC
5 .Place the remaining mix into a piping bag, once the cupcakes have cooled pipe on the top and place in the fridge to set

Brazilian Pineapple

Servings: 2

Ingredients:

- 1 small pineapple, cut into spears
- 100g brown sugar
- 2 tsp cinnamon
- 3 tbsp melted butter

Directions:

1 .Mix the brown sugar and cinnamon together in a small bowl
2 .Brush the pineapple with melted butter
3 .Sprinkle with the sugar and cinnamon
4 .Heat the air fryer to 200ºC
5 .Cook the pineapple for about 10 minutes

Chocolate Shortbread Balls

Servings: 9

Ingredients:

- 175g butter
- 75g caster sugar
- 250g plain flour
- 2 tsp vanilla essence
- 9 chocolate chunks
- 2 tbsp cocoa powder

Directions:

1 .Preheat the air fryer to 180ºC
2 .Add the flour, sugar and cocoa to a bowl and mix well
3 .Rub in the butter and vanilla then knead into a smooth dough
4 .Divide the mix into 9, place a chunk of chocolate in each piece and form into balls covering the chocolate
5 .Place the balls in the air fryer and cook at 180ºC for 8 mins then a further 6 mins at 160ºC

Thai Fried Bananas

Servings: 8

Ingredients:

- 4 ripe bananas
- 2 tbsp flour
- 2 tbsp rice flour
- 2 tbsp cornflour
- 2 tbsp desiccated coconut
- Pinch salt
- ½ tsp baking powder
- ½ tsp cardamon powder

Directions:

1 .Place all the dry ingredients in a bowl and mix well. Add a little water at a time and combine to form a batter
2 .Cut the bananas in half and then half again length wise
3 .Line the air fryer with parchment paper and spray with cooking spray
4 .Dip each banana piece in the batter mix and place in the air fryer
5 .Cook at 200ºC for 10 -15 minutes turning halfway
6 .Serve with ice cream

Brownies

Servings: 6

Ingredients:

- 25g melted butter
- 50g sugar
- 1 egg
- ½ tsp vanilla
- 25g flour
- 3 tbsp cocoa
- ⅛ tsp baking powder
- ⅛ tsp salt

Directions:

1 .Preheat the air fryer to 165°C
2 .Add all the wet ingredients to a bowl and combine.
3 .Add the dry ingredients and mix well
4 .Place the batter into a prepared pan and cook in the air fryer for 13 minutes

Chocolate Cake

Servings: 2

Ingredients:

- 3 eggs
- 75ml sour cream
- 225g flour
- 150g sugar
- 2 tsp vanilla extract
- 25g cocoa powder
- 1 tsp baking powder
- ½ tsp baking soda

Directions:

1 .Preheat the air fryer to 160°C
2 .Mix all the ingredients together in a bowl
3 .Pour into a greased baking tin
4 .Place into the air fryer and cook for 25 minutes
5 .Allow to cool and ice with chocolate frosting

Chocolate Dipped Biscuits

Servings: 6

Ingredients:

- 225g self raising flour
- 100g sugar
- 100g butter
- 50g milk chocolate
- 1 egg beaten
- 1 tsp vanilla essence

Directions:

1 .Add the flour, butter and sugar to a bowl and rub together
2 .Add the egg and vanilla, mix to form a dough
3 .Split the dough into 6 and form into balls
4 .Place in the air fryer cook at 180ºC for 15 minutes
5 .Melt the chocolate, dip the cooked biscuits into the chocolate and half cover

Zebra Cake

Servings: 6

Ingredients:

- 115g butter
- 2 eggs
- 100g caster sugar
- 1 tbsp cocoa powder
- 100g self raising flour
- 30ml milk
- 1tsp vanilla

Directions:

1 .Preheat air fryer to 160ºC
2 .Line a 6 inch baking tin
3 .Beat together the butter and sugar until light and fluffy
4 .Add eggs one at a time then add the vanilla and milk
5 .Add the flour and mix well
6 .Divide the mix in half
7 .Add cocoa powder to half the mix and mix well
8 .Add a scoop of each of the batters at a time until it's all in the tin, place in the air fryer and cook for 30 minutes

Apple Pie

Servings: 2

Ingredients:

- 1 packet of ready made pastry
- 1 apple, chopped
- 2 tsp lemon juice
- 1 tsp cinnamon
- 2 tbsp sugar
- ½ tsp vanilla extract
- 1 tbsp butter
- 1 beaten egg
- 1 tbsp raw sugar

Directions:

1 .Preheat the air fryer to 160ºC
2 .Line a baking tin with pastry
3 .Mix the apple, lemon juice, cinnamon, sugar and vanilla in a bowl
4 .Pour the apple mix into the tin with the pastry, top with chunks of butter
5 .Cover with a second piece of pastry, place three slits in the top of the pastry
6 .Brush the pastry with beaten egg and sprinkle with raw sugar
7 .Place in the air fryer and cook for 30 minutes

Melting Moments

Servings: 9

Ingredients:

- 100g butter
- 75g caster sugar
- 150g self raising flour
- 1 egg
- 50g white chocolate
- 3 tbsp desiccated coconut
- 1 tsp vanilla essence

Directions:

1 .Preheat the air fryer to 180ºC
2 .Cream together the butter and sugar, beat in the egg and vanilla
3 .Bash the white chocolate into small pieces
4 .Add the flour and chocolate and mix well
5 .Roll into 9 small balls and cover in coconut
6 .Place in the air fryer and cook for 8 minutes and a further 6 minutes at 160ºC

Christmas Biscuits

Servings: 8

Ingredients:

- 225g self raising flour
- 100g caster sugar
- 100g butter
- Juice and rind of orange
- 1 egg beaten
- 2 tbsp cocoa
- 2 tsp vanilla essence
- 8 pieces dark chocolate

Directions:

1 .Preheat the air fryer to 180ºC
2 .Rub the butter into the flour. Add the sugar, vanilla, orange and cocoa mix well
3 .Add the egg and mix to a dough
4 .Split the dough into 8 equal pieces
5 .Place a piece of chocolate in each piece of dough and form into a ball covering the chocolate
6 .Place in the air fryer and cook for 15 minutes

Apple And Cinnamon Puff Pastry Pies

Servings: 8

Ingredients:

- 4 tbsp butter
- 4 tbsp white sugar
- 2 tbsp brown sugar
- 1 tsp cinnamon
- 1 tsp nutmeg
- 1 tsp salt
- 4 apples, peeled and diced
- 2 large sheets puff pastry
- 1 egg

Directions:

1 .Preheat the air fryer to 180 °C / 350 °F. Remove the mesh basket from the machine and line it with parchment paper.
2 .In a bowl, whisk together the butter, white sugar, brown sugar, cinnamon, nutmeg, and salt.
3 .Place the apples in a heatproof baking dish and coat them in the butter and sugar mixture. Transfer to the air fryer and cook for 10 minutes.
4 .Meanwhile, roll out the pastry on a clean, floured surface. Cut the sheets into 8 equal parts.
5 .Once the apples are hot and softened, evenly spread the mixture between the pastry sheets. Fold the sheets over to cover the apple and gently press the edges using a fork or your fingers to seal the mixture in.
6 .Beat the egg in a bowl and use a brush to coat the top of each pastry sheet.
7 .Carefully transfer the filled pastry sheets to the prepared air fryer basket, close the lid, and cook for 10 minutes until the pastry is golden and crispy.

Banana And Nutella Sandwich

Servings: 2

Ingredients:

- Softened butter
- 4 slices white bread
- 25g chocolate spread
- 1 banana

Directions:

1 .Preheat the air fryer to 185°C
2 .Spread butter on one side of all the bread slices
3 .Spread chocolate spread on the other side of each slice
4 .Add sliced banana to two slices of bread then add the other slice of bread to each
5 .Cut in half diagonally to form triangles
6 .Place in the air fryer and cook for 5 minutes turn over and cook for another 2 minutes

Lava Cakes

Servings: 4

Ingredients:

- 1 ½ tbsp self raising flour
- 3 ½ tbsp sugar
- 150g butter
- 150g dark chocolate, chopped
- 2 eggs

Directions:

1 .Preheat the air fryer to 175°C
2 .Grease 4 ramekin dishes
3 .Melt chocolate and butter in the microwave for about 3 minutes
4 .Whisk the eggs and sugar together until pale and frothy
5 .Pour melted chocolate into the eggs and stir in the flour
6 .Fill the ramekins ¾ full, place in the air fryer and cook for 10 minutes

Banana Maple Flapjack

Servings: 9

Ingredients:

- 100 g/7 tablespoons butter (or plant-based spread if you wish)
- 75 g/5 tablespoons maple syrup
- 2 ripe bananas, mashed well with the back of a fork
- 1 teaspoon vanilla extract
- 240 g/2½ cups rolled oats/ quick-cooking oats

Directions:

1 .Gently heat the butter and maple syrup in a medium saucepan over a low heat until melted. Stir in the mashed banana, vanilla and oats and combine all ingredients. Pour the flapjack mixture into a 15 x 15-cm/6 x 6-in. baking pan and cover with foil.

2 .Preheat the air-fryer to 200ºC/400ºF.

3 .Add the baking pan to the preheated air-fryer and air-fry for 12 minutes, then remove the foil and cook for a further 4 minutes to brown the top. Leave to cool before cutting into 9 squares.

APPENDIX : Recipes Index

A

Air Fried Maple Chicken Thighs 38
Air Fryer Cheese Sandwich 59
Air Fryer Tuna 45
Apple And Cinnamon Puff Pastry Pies 70
Apple Pie 68
Asparagus & Steak Parcels 27

B

Bacon Wrapped Chicken Thighs 32
Baked Panko Cod 49
Banana And Nutella Sandwich 71
Banana Maple Flapjack 72
Beef Stuffed Peppers 29
Beef Wellington 25
Brazilian Pineapple 64
Breaded Bone-in Pork Chops 21
Breakfast Doughnuts 13
Breakfast Sausage Burgers 17
Broccoli Cheese 61
Brownies 66

C

Cajun Prawn Skewers 49
Camembert & Soldiers 58
Charred Chicken Breasts 33
Chicken And Cheese Chimichangas 39
Chicken Balls, Greek-style 37
Chicken Kiev 36
Chicken Tikka Masala 39
Chicken Tikka 38
Chickpea And Sweetcorn Falafel 57
Chilli Lime Tilapia 44
Chocolate Cake 66
Chocolate Dipped Biscuits 67
Chocolate Shortbread Balls 65
Christmas Biscuits 69
Copycat Burger 23

Copycat Fish Fingers 48
Courgette Burgers 56
Courgette Fries 14
Crispy Nacho Prawns 51
Crunchy Chicken Tenders 37
Crunchy Fish 45

D

Delicious Breakfast Casserole 17

E

Easy Air Fryer Sausage 18
Easy Cheese & Bacon Toasties 12
Egg & Bacon Breakfast Cups 16

F

Flat Mushroom Pizzas 59
French Toast Slices 15

G

Garlic Butter Salmon 51
Garlic Tilapia 50
Garlic-parsley Prawns 44
Grain-free Chicken Katsu 40

H

Hamburgers With Feta 28
Hawaiian Chicken 41
Healthy Breakfast Bagels 14
Healthy Stuffed Peppers 13
Homemade Crispy Pepperoni Pizza 26
Honey Sriracha Salmon 47

K

Key Lime Cupcakes 64

L

Lava Cakes 71
Lentil Burgers 61

M

Macaroni & Cheese Quiche 54
Mahi Fish Tacos 46
Meatballs In Tomato Sauce 21
Meatloaf 23
Melting Moments 69
Mexican Breakfast Burritos 16
Muhammara 19
Mushrooms Stuffed With Crab 50
Mustard Glazed Pork 24

N

Nashville Chicken 42

O

Onion Dumplings 58
Oozing Baked Eggs 15

P

Pakoras 60
Pizza Chicken Nuggets 34
Pork Belly With Crackling 30
Pork Chops With Sprouts 22
Pork Schnitzel 25
Potato & Chorizo Frittata 18
Potato Fries 12

R

Ranch Style Fish Fillets 48
Raspberry Breakfast Pockets 11
Ratatouille 62
Ravioli Air Fryer Style 56
Roast Beef 22
Roast Cauliflower & Broccoli 60
Roast Vegetables 62
Roasted Cauliflower 54

S

Salt & Pepper Calamari 47
Smoky Chicken Breast 33
Spinach And Egg Air Fryer Breakfast Muffins 55
Steak Popcorn Bites 28
Sticky Chicken Tikka Drumsticks 41

T

Tandoori Salmon 52
Thai Fried Bananas 65
Traditional Pork Chops 24
Turkey Cutlets In Mushroom Sauce 35

W

Whole Chicken 35
Wholegrain Pitta Chips 11

Z

Zebra Cake 67
Zesty Fish Fillets 52

Printed in Great Britain
by Amazon

18355816R00045